Personal Life Skills Printables Workbook:
for Students with Autism
&
Similar Special Needs

What's Included...	Page

Personal Skills
Printables Workbook
By: Autism Classroom

autismCLASSROOM.com

Personal Skills
Printables Workbook
By: Autism Classroom

autismCLASSROOM.com

Personal Information

This page is intentionally blank.

Name:_____

My Name

It is important to recognize your name when you see it and when you hear it.

What is
your name?

My name is

Teachers: Print the student's first name in one box and last name in the second box.

This page is intentionally blank.

Name:_____

I Know My Phone Number

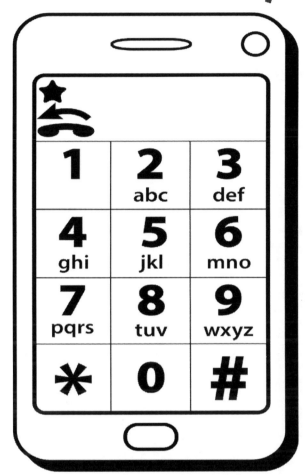

Point to the numbers in your phone number. Then cut and paste the numbers below to show your phone number.

My Phone Number

0	1	2	3	4	5	6	7	8	9
0	1	2	3	4	5	6	7	8	9
0	1	2	3	4	5	6	7	8	9

Teachers, if needed, write the number in the box and have students match to the same number.

This page is intentionally blank.

Name:_____

Address

Directions: Add the street number of your house and your school.

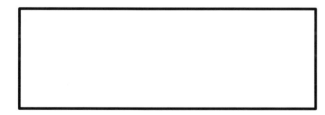

1	2	3	4	5	6	7	8	9	0
1	2	3	4	5	6	7	8	9	0
1	2	3	4	5	6	7	8	9	0

Adults: Write in the street name for the students.

This page is intentionally blank.

Name:_____

School

These are the many items we find at school. Glue the words in the correct spot.

pencil sharpener	board
pencil	backpack
chair	bulletin board
sink	door

This page is intentionally blank.

Name:_____

My Teacher

My teacher helps me to learn new things. My teacher makes sure I am safe at school. My teacher wants me to be happy. When I am at school, I pay attention to my teacher.

Check off the school behaviors after you read each one.

 I look.

 I listen.

I follow directions.

Spell the word teacher.

t h a c e e r

This page is intentionally blank.

Name:_____

Emergency Contact

In case of an emergency, here are things people can do.

Match the word to the picture.

Call 911.

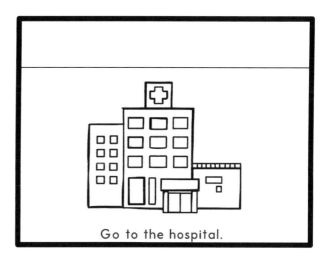

Go to the hospital.

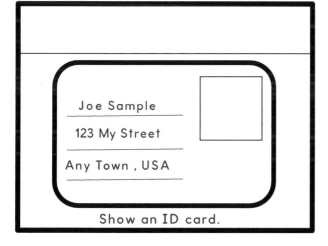

Show an ID card.

Raise hand to tell an adult.

911

hospital

identification card

raise hand to tell an adult

This page is intentionally blank.

Identification Card

Create your own identification card.

| Picture |

_____
Name

_____
Grade

_____
Classroom

✂

1 2 3 4 5 6 7 8 9

1 2 3 4 5 6 7 8 9

1 2 3 4 5 6 7 8 9

This page is intentionally blank.

My Birthday

Circle the month of your birthday.

JANUARY   FEBRUARY   MARCH   APRIL

MAY   JUNE   JULY   AUGUST

SEPTEMBER   OCTOBER   NOVEMBER   DECEMBER

Mark the number of your birthday.

1 2 3 4 5 6 7 8 9 10 11
12 13 14 15 16 17 18 19
20 21 22 23 24 25 26
27 28 29 30 31

Finish the sentence.

My birthday is _____ .

This page is intentionally blank.

How Old Are You?

Directions: Count the numbers on the page. Tell how old you are.

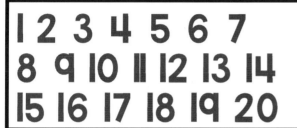

1	2	3	4	5	6	7
8	9	10	11	12	13	14
15	16	17	18	19	20	

How old are you?

I am ___ years old.

1	2	3	4	5	6	7	8	9	10
11	12	13	14	15	16	17	18	19	20

This page is intentionally blank.

Name:_____

Family

**Directions: Trace the words.
Draw a line from the word to
the picture.**

mom

dad

brother

sister

baby

This page is intentionally blank.

Name:_____

Siblings

Directions: Cut out the pictures. Next, fill out the chart.

brother	
sister	
baby	

I have

____ sisters

____ brothers

0	1	2	3	4	5	6	7	8
0	1	2	3	4	5	6	7	8

This page is intentionally blank.

Parents

Color by Code

Follow the directions to color the pictures.

1. Color the hair on each dad **brown**.
2. Color the shirt of the dad who is waving **blue**.
3. Color the shoes on the mom giving a hug **green**.
4. Color the hair of the mom who is sitting **yellow**.

This page is intentionally blank.

Name:_____

City Words

Directions: Match the words with the pictures. Then write in the name of your city.

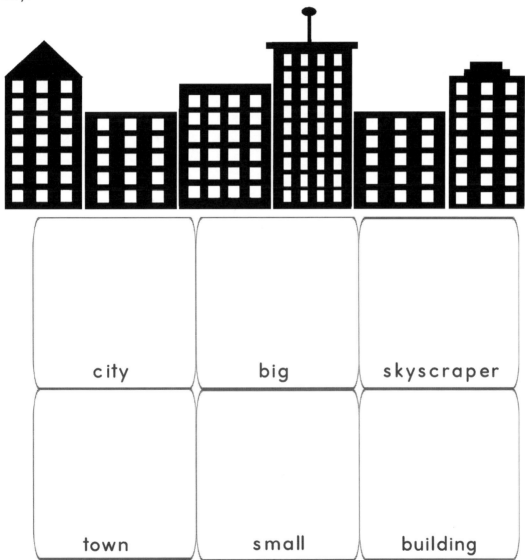

city	big	skyscraper
town	small	building

My city is _____●

city	big	town	building	small	skyscraper

This page is intentionally blank.

State

Directions: Count up to 50. Then, point to your state and color in your state.

(1) (2) (3) (4) (5) (6) (7) (8) (9) (10)

(11) (12) (13) (14) (15) (16) (17) (18) (19) (20)

(21) (22) (23) (24) (25) (26) (27) (28) (29) (30)

(31) (32) (33) (34) (35) (36) (37) (38) (39) (40)

(41) (42) (43) (44) (45) (46) (47) (48) (49) (50)

My state.

Directions: Glue in the letters that make the abbreviation for your state.

This page is intentionally blank.

Personal Management

Name:_____

Tie Shoes

Tips for Tying a Shoe

1. Lace shoes correctly.
2. Hold both laces
3. Cross the laces.
4. Put one lace through the middle.
5. Pull both laces tight.
6. Make a two loops.
7. Tie the loops to make a bow.
8. Pull tight.

Trace the word.

Circle the pictures with shoes on.
Underline the pictures with shoes off.

Draw a line to the same shoes.

Putting on My Coat

How To Put On A Coat

1. Hold your coat with one hand.

2. Slip the other hand into the sleeve.

3. Pull the coat up on your shoulder.

4. Reach the other arm behind your back.

5. Put that arm through the other sleeve.

Practice putting on a coat, sweater or jacket.

up	down	Put on	Take off
⬆	⬇		

Cut and match the correct phrase to the image/symbol.

| Zip the coat up. | Put on the coat. | Take the coat off. | Zip the coat down. |

This page is intentionally blank.

 # Hang Coat

When people take off their coat, they need a place to put the coat. Most people put their coat in a place where they can find it when it is time to put the coat on again. Some people put their coat in a locker. Some people use other ways to hang their coat.

Directions: Write the word.

locker

locker

Check yes or no for each statement.

WHEN SHOULD JANE TAKE OFF HER COAT?	When she walks into the house.	When she comes into the classroom at school.	When she is going into the snow.	At her locker.
	Yes No	Yes No	Yes No	Yes No

Directions: Cut and paste. Use the answers at the bottom of the page.

Where can you place your coat?

1	2	3

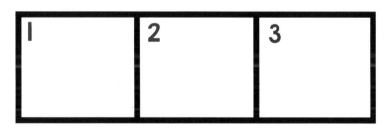

This page is intentionally blank.

Buttoning Items

Practice buttoning a shirt.

Connect the buttons with a line.

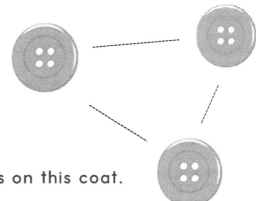

Count the buttons on this coat.

How many buttons are on the coat?

1 2 3 4 5 6 7 8 9 10

Directions: Write the word.

button button

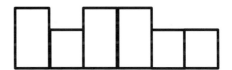

This page is intentionally blank.

Name:_____

Brushing Teeth

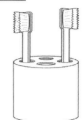

Steps in Toothbrushing

1.

2.

3.

4.

5.

Trace the words.

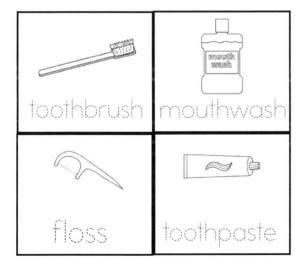

toothbrush   mouthwash

floss   toothpaste

Directions: Cut, then paste in order at the top of the page.

Get toothpaste. ①

Squeeze toothpaste on toothbrush. ②

Place toothbrush in mouth on your teeth. ③

Brush teeth. ④

Rinse. ⑤

This page is intentionally blank.

Name:_____

Washing Hands

Shya sneezed and needed to wash her hands. First, she looked for the soap. Next, she turned on the water and washed her hands. After that, she used a dryer to dry her hands. When that didn't dry them, she used a towel.

Steps for Drying Hands

get paper towel   wipe hands on towel   throw in trash

Cut and paste under the correct picture.

soap   water

dry hands   towel

This page is intentionally blank.

47

Name:_____

Morning Bathroom Sequence

These kids are showing a morning sequence for getting ready for school. Look at the pictures that are in order from top to bottom. Then, place the ordinal number beside the picture to order from 1st to 6th to show the order.

1st

3rd

2nd

4th

6th

5th

This page is intentionally blank.

49

Name:_____

Evening Bathroom Sequence

Directions: Cut out the pictures and glue them into the correct box.

Take bath or shower.		
Put on pajamas.		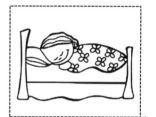
Brush teeth.		
Wash face.		
Go to sleep.		

This page is intentionally blank.

Name:_____

Staying Safe - Staying with the Group

Georgia is trying to improve her personal management skills. She knows one thing she can do to stay safe at school is to walk in line. She wants to know what else will help her stay safe at school. What could Georgia do to stay safe at school?

Cut and place with the correct picture.

Use a count down board.	Use picture cards.	Follow her schedule.	Stay with the group.
Look at the teacher.	Do her work.	Fall on the floor.	Play with her locker.

This page is intentionally blank.

Name:_____

 # My Self, My Health

There are many items that people use to stay healthy.
Some of those items are
shampoo, deodorant, floss, nail clippers and a comb.

<u>Directions:</u> Draw a line from one item to its match.

Optional: Teachers show the real objects or internet photos of these items.

Eating at Mealtime

Directions: Mark the correct word that goes with the picture.

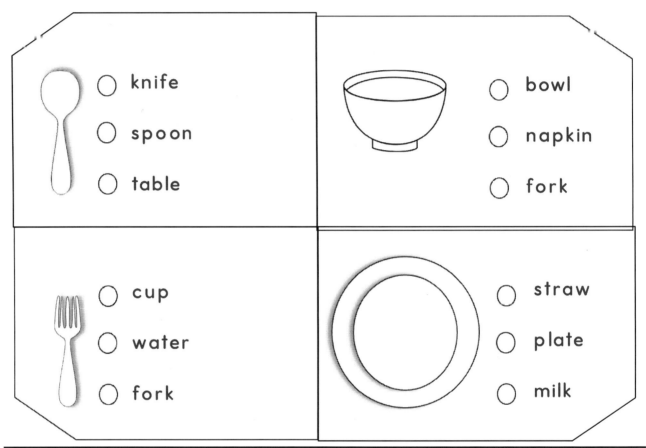

- ○ knife
- ○ spoon
- ○ table

- ○ bowl
- ○ napkin
- ○ fork

- ○ cup
- ○ water
- ○ fork

- ○ straw
- ○ plate
- ○ milk

School

At school kids finish eating, pick up their lunch tray and throw away the garbage.

Directions: Draw a line from the tray to the trash can.

Home

At home, kids finish eating, pick up their plate and put it in the sink or the dishwasher.

Directions: Draw a line from the plate and cup to the sink.

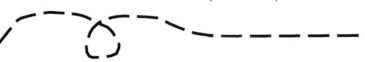

Name:_____

When to Use a Utensil or Eat with Your Hands

Look at these kids. Point to what they are using to eat their food.

use a spoon

use a fork

use your hands

Directions: Cut out words on the right side of the paper. Match the words into the correct column.

hands	fork	spoon

Optional: Teachers show pictures or internet photos of these items. (4 hands, 3 spoon, 2 fork)

✂

sandwich

yogurt

soup

ice cream cone

chips

hot dog

cereal

pie

spaghetti

This page is intentionally blank.

Name:_____

Eating Slow and Chewing All Food

Use a bowl or small container of cotton balls, cut pieces of paper or dry cereal. Have students use a spoon to scoop these items into another container. Practice scooping fast, then slow. Next, pretend to make chewing motions with your mouth. Have students imitate a fast chewing motion, then a slow chewing motion, while pointing to fast and slow.

5 times

Scoop

5 times

Fast

Slow

Chew

Next, have students use a spoon to practice making small scoops and big scoops.

5 times

5 times

Scoop

Small

Big

Sarita is having trouble when she eats. Sometimes she moves so quick that the food gets on her shirt. To stop this from happening, how should she eat?

(Fast)   (Slow)

How should she scoop her food?

(Small)   (Big)

This page is intentionally blank.

59

Name:_____

Getting Dressed

Directions: Sequence the steps for getting dressed.

Mark is sleeping but he needs to get up and get ready for the day. His mom says "Time to get dressed." Mark needs to put on his pants, put on his shirt, put on his socks and put on his shoes. Can you help show the correct pictures in the correct order for Mark to get dressed?

Steps to Getting Dressed

1	2	3	4

Put on pants.

Put on shoes.

Put on shirt.

Put on socks.

This page is intentionally blank.

Name:_____

Routine for Using the Bathroom

Directions: Cut on the dashed lines. Match the picture to the correct statement.

Sit on the toilet and go to the bathroom. Wipe self with toilet tissue.

Pull up underclothes and pants. Flush the toilet.

Wash hands.

Dry hands with a hand dryer or paper towels.

This page is intentionally blank.

Name:_____

Opening Containers

Directions: Mark the correct answer to tell if each item is open or closed.

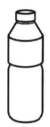

 open  closed

 open closed

open closed

 open closed

Write in the word open.

open

open

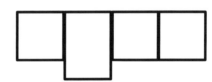

Write in the word close.

close

close

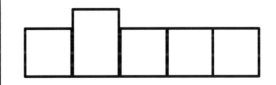

Bonus: Have students practice opening empty containers.

This page is intentionally blank.

Knowing My Environment

Directions: Cut and paste the pictures in the correct box.

AROUND THE HOUSE

What room do these belong in?

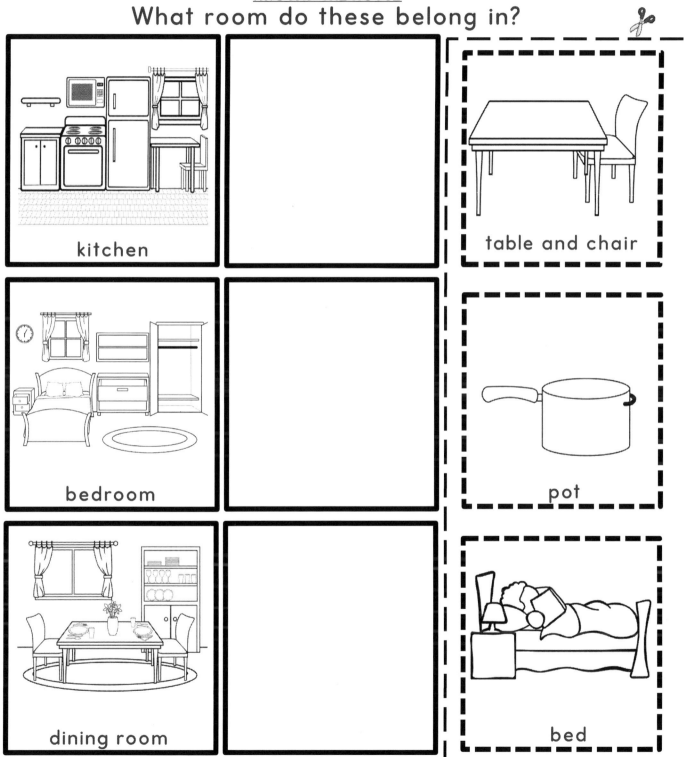

kitchen

table and chair

bedroom

pot

dining room

bed

This page is intentionally blank.

Name:_____

Stay with the Group,

Don't Wander

Shirley is working with the group but she hears something in the hall. What should she do? Color the circle that shows what she should do.

Run to the hallway.

Cry.

Push through the door.

Sulk.

Stay with the group.

Restaurant Dining

○ menu
○ table
○ corn

Kelly and Clark love dining at a restaurant. When they are there, they see many things. Mark the correct definition for the people and things they see at a restaurant.

○ water
○ waitress
○ light

○ restaurant
○ hospital
○ school

○ cook
○ chef
○ waiter

RESTAURANT RULES

Trace the words in the sentences.

1. Use an inside voice.

2. Wait patiently for your food.

3. Only eat your food.

4. Keep your food on the table.

Name:_____

Fast Food Dining

Trace the lines to show the process for ordering fast food. Point to the words in each step of the process.

Walk to the fast food counter.

Choose your food by pointing to it or saying its name.

Pay the money to the cashier.

Wait for your food to be cooked.

Find a place to sit and eat your food.

Family Gatherings

Directions: Trace inside the lines or write the words on the left. Draw a line or use glue and string to match the words to the correct picture.

G R A N D M A

| Grandma is giving me a hug. |

G R A N D P A

| Grandpa is looking at my new tablet with me. |

C O U S I N S

| My cousins are watching TV. |

A U N T

| My aunt is looking at my phone. |

U N C L E

| My uncle is taking pictures. |

Going to the Store

cart

Directions: Push the cart through the maze using a pencil or crayon.
Don't bump any food.

Start

Finish

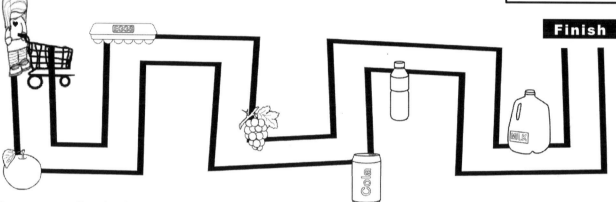

Directions: Finish the pattern.

Shop	Pay	Shop	Pay	Shop	

Directions: Finish the pattern.

Stay with the adult.	W a l k .	Stay with the adult.	W a l k .	Stay with the adult.	

Directions: Finish the pattern.

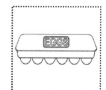 | W a l k | Pay

This page is intentionally blank.

Name:_____

Going to the Library

These students practice self-control when going to the library. They know that they must control their own actions and words when they are in the library. Color in the phrases that show what they do when they go to the library.

USE A VERY
QUIET
VOICE.

LISTEN TO
THE
LIBRARIAN.

CHECK OUT
BOOKS TO
BORROW.

USE
EARPHONES
WITH YOUR
COMPUTER.

KEEP YOUR
FEET ON
THE
FLOOR.

Count the books. Mark the answer.

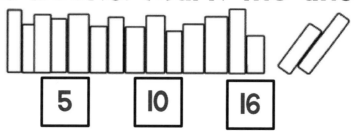

| 5 | 10 | 16 |

Personal Responsibility

YES or NO

Kitchen Skills

Is this done in the kitchen?

Directions: Glue the correct answer in the box.

Wash dishes.	
Put dishes away.	
Sweep the kitchen floor.	
Make the bed.	
Flush the toilet.	

What can we do in the kitchen?

○ garden

○ cook

○ sleep

YES	YES	NO	NO	YES

This page is intentionally blank.

Name:_____

More Kitchen Skills

Read or point to the name of each item. Mark the correct answer to show if the item is open or closed.

Microwave

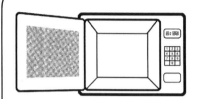 Open

Closed

 Open

Closed

Stove

 Open

Closed

 Open

Closed

Refrigerator

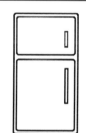 Open

Closed

 Open

Closed

Cabinet

 Open

Closed

 Open

Closed

This page is intentionally blank.

Name:_____

Microwave

Microwaves can cook food fast. Some people use them to make popcorn, to heat up dinner and for many other foods. Cut and paste the words to label the correct parts of a microwave.

2 minutes for popcorn

Parts of the microwave

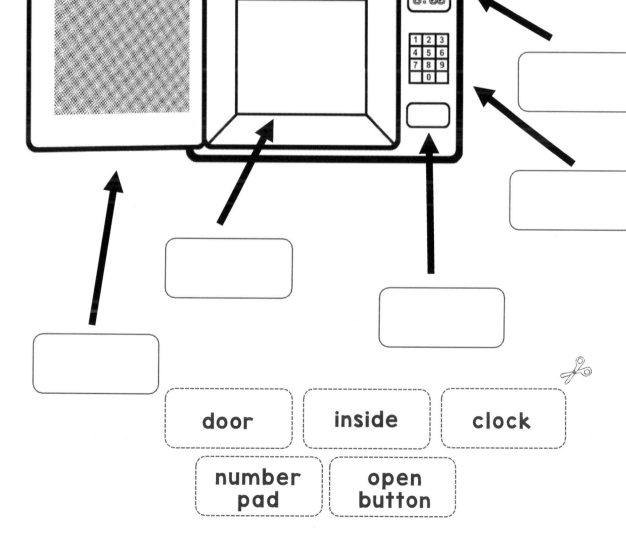

door   inside   clock

number pad   open button

This page is intentionally blank.

What Goes in the Refrigerator? What Goes in the Freezer?

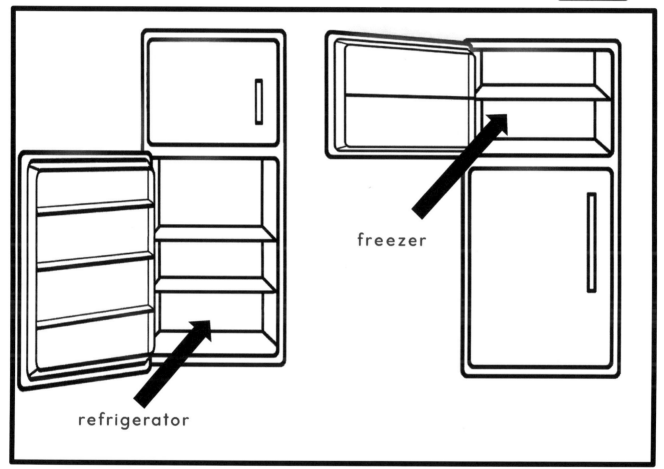

freezer

refrigerator

Put 5 refrigerator items in the refrigerator. Put 2 freezer items in the freezer.

milk   water   soda   ice cream   eggs   ice tray   butter

This page is intentionally blank.

Name:_____

Toaster

Directions: Trace the words of foods that can go in a toaster.

bagel

bread

french toast

waffle

pancake

Draw a line from the word to the picture.

| knife | butter | bread | plate | jelly |

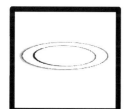    

Personal Life Skills Printables

Name:_____

Label the Chores

Directions: Draw a line from the name of the chore to the picture of the chore.

Washing the dog.	Dusting.	Ironing.

Directions: Check the box that tells the name of this chore.

Vacuum

The vacuum can be loud. It's ok. The vacuum is just cleaning up dirt from the carpet. Don't worry, the vacuum won't clean up people, but it will clean up any small toys that are left on the floor.

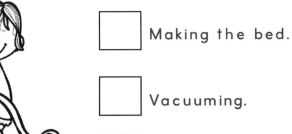

☐ Making the bed.

☐ Vacuuming.

☐ Washing dishes.

Bonus: Pretend to do the chore.

Name:_____

How to Make a Bed

Directions: Put the steps in order
for making a bed.
How can Carol make the bed?

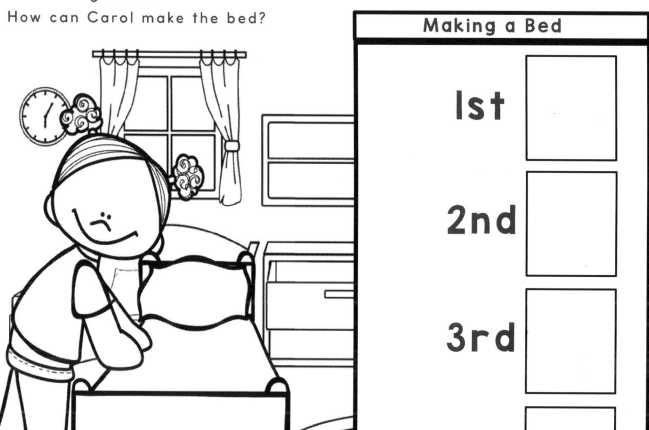

Making a Bed	
1st	
2nd	
3rd	
4th	

Pull up the blanket and smooth out wrinkles on the blanket.

Straighten the sheet by pulling the top sheet as far up as it will go.

Smooth out the wrinkles in the sheet with her hands.

Fluff pillow and place it at the top of the bed.

This page is intentionally blank.

Name:_____

Sweeping & Mopping

Directions: Read the instructions in the box.

Mark the chore that is the same.

same

same

different

different

Mark the chore that is **different**.

Directions: Read the sentences. Trace the words in the box.

 Sweep with a...

 broom

 Mop with a...

 mop and bucket

This page is intentionally blank.

Wiping Tables

Directions: Number the steps involved in wiping the table.

☐ Clear off the table.

☐ Get a sponge.

☐ Wet the sponge.

☐ Wipe the table.

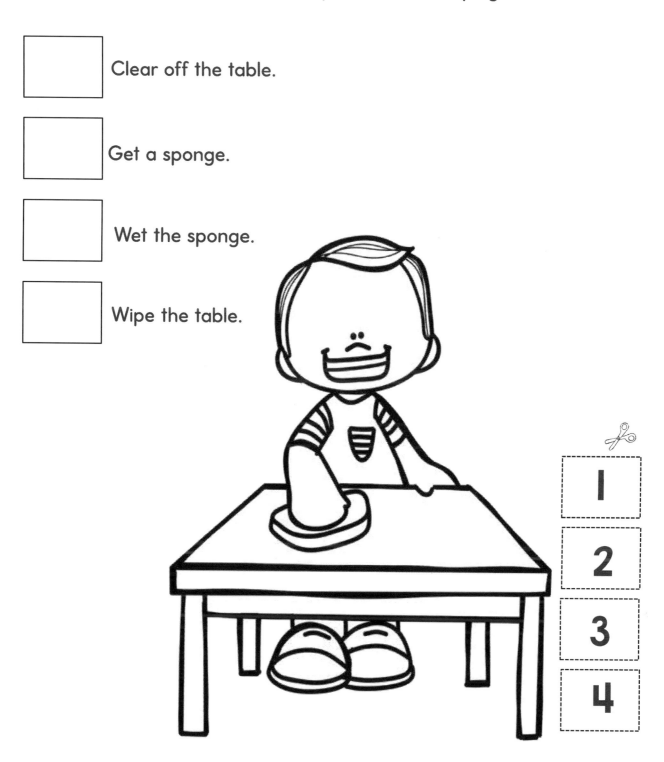

1

2

3

4

This page is intentionally blank.

Color in the words.

Cleaning Up Toys

When is a good time to clean up toys?

◯ Yes
◯ No

After I finish playing.

◯ Yes
◯ No

When I am going to do a different activity.

◯ Yes
◯ No

When I am sleeping.

What is this boy doing?

◯ Cleaning up

◯ Making a mess

Finish the Song

Clean up,
Clean up,
Everybody do
your share,
Clean up,
Clean up,

_____

WRITE IT !!!

clean up

This page is intentionally blank.

Name:_____

Washing Dishes

<u>Directions</u>: Read the sentences. Place the numbers of each step in the correct order.

☐ First, get a dishcloth and dish soap.

☐ Second, go to the sink.

☐ Third, wash the dishes in the sink.

☐ Fourth, rinse the dishes and dry the dishes.

☐ Fifth, put the dishes away.

Extension Activity: Practice washing a plastic cup in a tub of shallow water.

- -

[1] [2] [3] [4] [5]

This page is intentionally blank.

Name:_____

Setting the Table - page 1

Directions: Match the picture to the same picture.

spoon

fork

napkin

cup

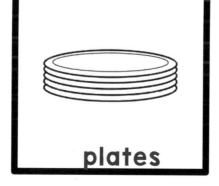

plates

table

This page is intentionally blank.

Name:_____

Setting the Table - page 2

spoon

fork

napkin

cup

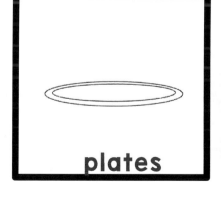

plates

table

This page is intentionally blank.

Name:_____

Washing Clothes- Opposites

Washing clothes shows us many opposites. Sometimes people have clothes that are dirty and then after they wash them, the clothes are clean. Sometimes, the washer is open and other times it is closed. Take a look at the filters, the clothes basket, the shirts and the washing machines and identity the opposites.

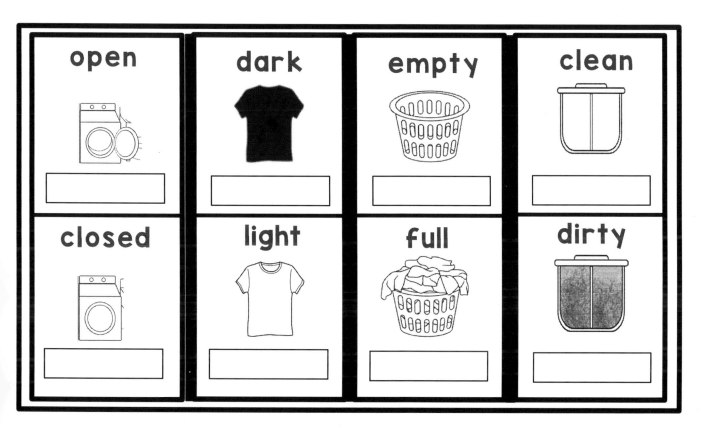

Directions: Cut out the words below and match them to the correct box with that same word.

This page Is intentionally blank.

Name:_____

Sorting Clothes

| Vocabulary |
| Pile |
| Folded |
| Basket |
| Clean |
| Dirty |

Directions: Color in the picture using the directions at the bottom of the page.

Clean   ## Dirty

LOOK FOR	DO
One clean shirt.	Color the shirt yellow.
A pile of clothes in a basket.	Color them blue.
One shirt with a stain.	Circle the stain.
11 clean, folded shirts.	Color them in rainbow colors.
A pile of clothes out of the basket.	Color them red.

Personal Life Skills Printables

Name:_____

What I Do in the Morning

These students get dressed in the morning, then they get ready for school.

Directions: Rainbow color the morning routine words, watch the example and pretend to do the action.

wake up   clothes   comb/brush hair

put on socks   shoes

Directions: Color by following the directions below.

Color all the boys shirts **black**.
Color the girl's hair brush **purple**.
Color the shoes **yellow**.
Color the socks **blue**.
Color the bed **brown**.

Name:_____

Getting Ready for Sleep

Directions: Draw a line from the picture to the same picture.

| Put on pajamas. | Brush my teeth. | Get in the bed. | Go to sleep. |

This page Is Intentionally blank.

Name:_____

Barber or Hair Salon

Directions: Describe the picture.

Buzzzzz

[ ]

[ ]

[ ]

[ ]

- -

The barber will use clippers to cut your hair, if you need a haircut. The clippers will make a buzzing sound.

The stylist will blow dry your hair using a hair dryer. The wind from the hair dryer will be warm.

The shampoo person will take you to the shampoo bowl, then have you sit while they wet your hair and add shampoo. They will clean it, then dry it with a towel.

The hair dresser will ask you to sit in the chair. She will use a comb and a brush. If you are getting your haircut, she will use scissors.

This page is intentionally blank.

Personal Trips

This page Is Intentionally blank.

Trips in the Community

Directions: Cut the images at the bottom of the page. Match them to the buildings you see in the community.

bank

car repair shop

post office

hospital

school

police station

This page is intentionally blank.

Name:_____

Community Buildings

Directions: Write the word on the line. Look for the real pictures in a magazine or draw your own picture of the community building.

↓ Your Drawing or Picture ↓

hospital

fire station

restaurant

school

This page Is Intentionally blank.

Name:_____

Vacation

airplane

Questions:

1. What is a vacation?

2. How do some people get to a vacation?

3. What can people do on a vacation?

Cut and paste in the correct answer.

An airplane.

Visit new places.

A chance to travel.

Go to school.

This page is intentionally blank.

Name:_____

Airplane Travel

○ train
○ airplane

○ pilot
○ doctor

Tips for Your Airplane Ride:
- Stay in your seat.
- Chew gum if it feels like the inside of your ear is hurting.
- The plane goes high and you will feel it go up.
- Wait for your turn to get inside of the plane.
- Follow directions when you are on a plane.

Directions: Mark the correct word to label the airplane related picture.

○ passenger
○ school

○ luggage
○ frame

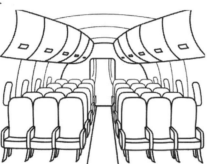

○ airplane cabin (inside of the airplane)
○ airplane wing (outside of the airplane)

○ nurse
○ flight attendant

○ jump rope

○ seatbelt

Airplane Word Search

Find the words in the words search.

wing
pilot
plane
captain
luggage

c	a	p	t	a	i	n	p
e	s	h	w	f	f	e	i
m	m	a	i	b	l	m	l
p	l	a	n	e	o	p	o
l	u	g	g	a	g	e	t

Personal Life Skills Printables

Name:_____

Preparing for a Trip Checklist

If you are going on a short trip or a long trip and need to pack, it helps to make a checklist. John needs to pack his bag for a long trip. Can you help him check off each item if you see a picture for that item.

<u>Directions:</u> Draw a check mark or a dot in the small square if the item is present.

☐	suitcase
☐	socks
☐	pants and shirt
☐	shoes
☐	hair supplies

Is John ready for his trip?
Does he have all of the items on his checklist?

yes   no

Name:_____

Ways to Travel

Trace the words. The draw a line to the picture that matches that word.

train

bus

car

plane

Name:_____

Hotels

Directions: Read each circle. Mark all of the circles that name people you see in a hotel.

Sometimes people go vacation or take a trip outside of their house. When they do, they can sometimes stay at a family members house, at a rented house or they can stay at a hotel. At a hotel, you can see many people in different occupations working on different jobs.

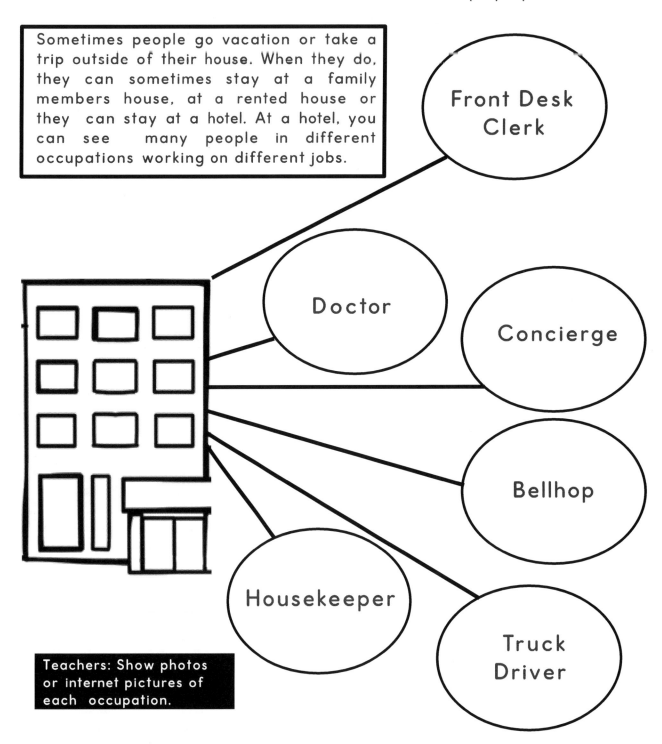

Front Desk Clerk

Doctor

Concierge

Bellhop

Housekeeper

Truck Driver

Teachers: Show photos or internet pictures of each occupation.

Movies

When people go to the movies, there is a routine. Read each box below to see the routine.

| Purchase tickets. |

| Buy popcorn. |

| Dispense drink. |

| Find a seat. |

| Watch previews of other movies on the screen. |

| The lights go out. It gets dark. |

| Everyone gets quiet. |

| Movie starts. |

| Watch the movie. |

Directions: Count the tickets. Color the tickets.

tickets

How many tickets?

1   2

Directions: Cut, then paste on the same words on the list above.

| Purchase tickets. |

| Buy popcorn. |

| Dispense drink. |

| Find a seat. |

| Watch previews of other movies on the screen. |

| The lights go out. It gets dark. |

| Everyone gets quiet. |

| Movie starts. |

| Watch the movie. |

This page Is Intentionally blank.

Name:_____

Going to Visit Family & Friends

Directions: Start at the van and trace the line to help Sam get to grandmom.

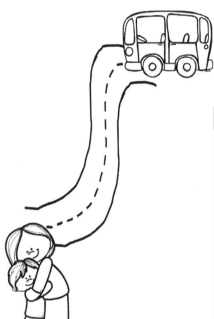

Reading a Calendar

Sometimes placing a visual symbol on a calendar can help people who are visual learners to remember what will happen during the month. Sam has a calendar that uses symbols.

February

Monday	Tuesday	Wednesday	Thursday	Friday	Saturday	Sunday
1	2	3	4	5	6	7
8	9	10	11	12	13 visit grandmom	14 visit grandmom
15	16	17	18	19	20 visit grandmom	21 visit grandmom
22	23	24	25	26	27	28

Read the calendar above.
What days does Sam go to visit grandma?

1	2	3	4	5	6	7	8	9	10	11
12	13	14	15	16	17	18	19			
20	21	22	23	24	25	26				
27	28	29	30	31						

Instead of staying home on February 6th, Sam learns that he will be going to a restaurant to get fries. Cut and paste the picture of restaurant below and place it in the correct box on the calendar.

This page is intentionally blank.

Personal Life Skills Printables

Parks

Name:_____

Directions: Match to the correct type of park.

nature center

amusement park

local park

nature center

amusement park

local park

This page Is Intentionally blank.

Name:_____

Amusement Parks

Teachers: Show a photo or internet picture of each of these items before completing the worksheet.

Directions: Dot a circle that shows your choice when you go to an amusement park.

ferris wheel
OR
roller coaster

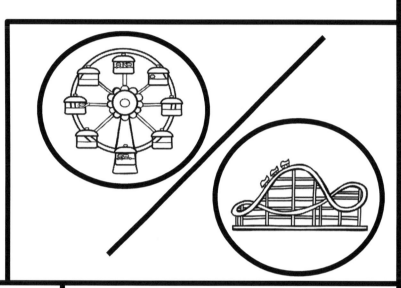

merry-go-round
OR
bouncy castle

cotton candy
OR
play games

This page is intentionally blank.

Name:_____

Beach Words Match Up

<u>Directions:</u> Cut the circles at the bottom of the page and match them to the circles at the top of the page.

This page is intentionally blank.

Name:_____

Splash! Water Fun

Some days there are trips that involve water and water play. What are some good rules to remember when you have a water play trip?

Sprinklers

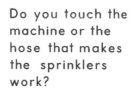

Do you touch the machine or the hose that makes the sprinklers work?

 YES   NO

Water balloons

Should you throw water balloons at someone's head?

 YES   NO

Water park

Do you stay with your family at the water park?

 YES   NO

Water hose

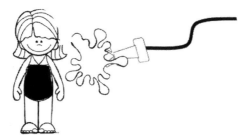

Should you run when using the water hose?

 YES   NO

Water slide

Should you take turns on the water slide?

 YES   NO

Special Thanks.

Thanks to the following artists for their wonderful clip art.

Educlips
Rossey's Jungle
Allison Fors
Ramona M Graphics

AutismClassroom.com offers books and resources for Special Education and General Education. We make materials to bring out the best in your students with autism and similar needs.

THANK YOU FOR YOUR PURCHASE.

 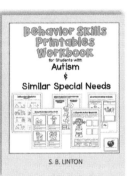  

 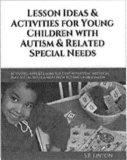  

Website: www.autismclassroom.com
Teachers Pay Teachers: www.TeachersPayTeachers.com/Store/Autism-Classroom
Instagram: www.Instagram.com/autismclassroom
Facebook: www.Facebook.com/Autism-Classroom-309583732914

Made in the USA
Columbia, SC
08 October 2024

43846530R00072